FOREWORD BY ALLISON D. MAHON

FOREVER LINKED

ERIC CARPENTER
SHERILL GRANT-CARPENTER

THIS IS A WRITTEN WORK BY
Eric Carpenter & Sherill Grant Carpenter
PUBLISHED BY DAUGHTERS OF DEBORAH PUBLISHING

This is a book based on the divinely inspired thoughts and life experiences of
Eric Carpenter & Sherill Grant Carpenter
All content therein is written as recalled and recounted by them.
All identities are used by permission or purposely omitted to protect the privacy of those living or dead.

Copyright© January 2025
By Eric Carpenter & Sherill Grant Carpenter

Published in the United States of America by
Eric Carpenter & Sherill Grant Carpenter
An imprint of
DAUGHTERS OF DEBORAH PUBLISHING

All rights reserved under International Copyright Law. Contents and cover may not be reproduced in whole or in part in any form without the author or publisher's written consent.
www.SGCMinistries.com

Library of Congress Cataloguing-In-Publication Number **PENDING**

ISBN 979-8-9920189-2-9

First Edition Printing
Printed in the United States of America
January 2025

Daughters of Deborah Publishing
1515 Lincoln Place
Second Floor
Brooklyn, NY 11213
www.AllisonMahonMinistries.com

In loving memory of
Constance Carpenter
April 7, 1942 - June 9, 2024
Earl Carpenter Sr.
Nov 8, 1937 - May 20, 2017

To my better half, my good thing! I love you!

Thank you for allowing me to partner with you in every way, and for loving me the way you do.

To my Mom and my Dad, you are now with The Lord, thank you for everything.

Most importantly thank you Lord for blessing our marriage and our children, and generations to come with a legacy of love for you and each other.

To my brother Earl I love and honor you. Thank you for being my best friend!

To my Dad and my Bishop, thank you and Mom for loving me and covering us in prayer always!

God gave me His best when He blessed me with you and Dr. Joy.

In loving memory of
Dr. Joy Grant
4-29-1951 to 9-4-2023

To my incredible parents,
Bishop Easton and Dr. Joy Grant,

Thank you for loving me unconditionally and leading me to Christ.
Your lives have been a shining example of a godly marriage, inspiring me and so many others.

Thank you for embracing my husband with love, and Daddy, thank you for the honor of giving me to him.

Mom, you exemplified what it means to be a Woman of God, a Proverbs 31 wife, and an extraordinary mother, grandmother and friend!

Your absence is deeply felt, but your tremendous impact and enduring legacy continue to inspire.

You and Daddy are the embodiment of
""Til death do us part."

The Foundation

25 Husbands, love your wives, just as Christ also loved the church and gave Himself for her, 26 that He might [a]sanctify and cleanse her with the washing of water by the word, 27 that He might present her to Himself a glorious church, not having spot or wrinkle or any such thing, but that she should be holy and without blemish. 28 So husbands ought to love their own wives as their own bodies; he who loves his wife loves himself. 29 For no one ever hated his own flesh, but nourishes and cherishes it, just as the Lord does the church. 30 For we are members of His body, [b]of His flesh and of His bones. 31 "For this reason a man shall leave his father and mother and be joined to his wife, and the two shall become one flesh." 32 This is a great mystery, but I speak concerning Christ and the church. 33 Nevertheless let each one of you in particular so love his own wife as himself, and let the wife see that she respects her husband.

Ephesians 5:25-33

TABLE OF CONTENTS

ACKNOWLEDGEMENTS	10
FOREWORD	12
INTRODUCTION	14
• DAY 1 A FOUNDATION OF LOVE	18
• DAY 2 COMMUNICATION IN UNITY	20
• DAY 3 STRENGTHENING TRUST	22
• DAY 4 SERVING ONE ANOTHER	24
• DAY 5 PRAYING FOR WISDOM	26
• DAY 6 BUILDING PATIENCE	28
• DAY 7 EMBRACING FORGIVENESS	30
WEEK ONE ACTIVITIES & RECAP	32
• DAY 8 SPIRITUAL GROWTH TOGETHER	34
• DAY 9 STRENGTH IN CHALLENGES	36
• DAY 10 CELEBRATING DIFFERENCES	38
• DAY 11 GROWING IN GRATITUDE	40
• DAY 12 FACING FEARS TOGETHER	42
• DAY 13 FINANCIAL STEWARDSHIP	44
• DAY 14 PROTECTING THE COVENANT	46

TABLE OF CONTENTS

WEEK TWO ACTIVITIES & RECAP 48

- DAY 15 RENEWING COMMITMENT 50
- DAY 16 WALKING IN FAITH TOGETHER 52
- DAY 17 ENCOURAGING ONE ANOTHER 54
- DAY 18 PROTECTING EACH OTHERS HEARTS 56
- DAY 19 HONORING EACH OTHER 58
- DAY 20 LOVING THROUGH CHALLENGES 60
- DAY 21 RESTORING JOY 62

WEEK THREE ACTIVITIES & RECAP 64

- DAY 22 CULTIVATING PEACE 66
- DAY 23 NURTURING INTIMACY 68
- DAY 24 TRUSTING GOD'S TIMING 70
- DAY 25 FAITHFULNESS IN ALL THINGS 72
- DAY 26 HEALING THROUGH PRAYER 74
- DAY 27 STRENGTHENING UNITY 76
- DAY 28 OVERCOMING TEMPTATIONS 78

WEEK FOUR ACTIVITIES & RECAP 80

- DAY 29 LEAVING A LEGACY OF LOVE 82

TABLE OF CONTENTS

- **DAY 30 RENEWING HOPE**   84
- **DAY 31 A PRAYER OF BLESSING**   86

    WEEK FIVE ACTIVITIES & RECAP   88

ENDORSEMENTS   89

OUR NOTES   91

ABOUT THE AUTHORS   116

Acknowledgements

First and foremost, we give all glory to God for the grace, wisdom, and love that made this devotional possible. Writing together as husband and wife has been a joyful journey filled with prayer, honesty, laughter, and growth.

We lovingly honor our parents, Bishop Easton and the late Dr. Joy Grant, whose lives have been powerful examples of what it means to serve in marriage and ministry. Their unwavering faith and commitment laid the foundation upon which we now build.

To our marriage mentors, Overseer Keith and Pastor Andrea Heyward, thank you for your godly counsel, encouragement, and modeling what a thriving, Christ-centered marriage looks like. Your wisdom has shaped our walk together in immeasurable ways.

To our amazing children, Danielle, Joshua, Matasha, Jordyn, Joy, and our granddaughter Dasean, our hearts are full of prayers that God will bless each of you with a spouse who loves Him first and loves you deeply. Always remember: Marriage still works when Christ is at the center.

To our cherished couple friends, thank you for the community. Always remember that prayer and intentional pursuits never go out of style. Let us continue to date, grow, pray together, and inspire each other. We love you and are always lifting you in prayer.

A heartfelt thank you to Bishop Marvin and Pastor Veda McCoy for creating a safe and Spirit-led environment for couples to thrive. We appreciate your trust in allowing us to serve in this sacred area of ministry; we are truly honored.

To our beloved mentors, Pastor Allison, thank you for graciously writing the foreword and for being a constant blessing to our family. We love and honor you, Bishop Rufus Mahon, and our nephew Josiah. Your impact and encouragement mean the world to us.

To Dr. Angel Thompson and The LEGNA Agency, thank you for publishing this project with excellence and care. Your vision and professionalism have brought this dream to life with beauty and purpose.

To my bestie and prayer partner, Tori, thank you for the nights you stayed up travailing with me in prayer, believing in me, and recognizing the oil on my life. Your love and support have been a lifeline. We love you dearly.

To our godchildren, Gam and Carly Duret, we love you and are so grateful for the opportunity to pour into your marriage. We are incredibly proud of both of you and our beautiful grand-babies. No eye has seen, no ear has heard, and no mind has imagined what God has prepared for you. The best is truly yet to come.

Lastly, to every married couple that will read this book-be intentional about spending time together in prayer and God's word!

With hearts full of gratitude,

Eric & Sherill Carpenter

Foreword

Forever Linked devotional will be a "God wink" for many couples. At a time when so many "Christian" marriages are failing or severely tested. This devotional could not have come at a better time. This devotional is not just a collection of words; it is a heartfelt invitation to cultivate a deeper relationship with each other and with God.

Marriage is a divine gift, a beautiful tapestry woven with love, faith, and intentionality. It is a partnership that reflects God's grace and challenges us to grow in ways we never thought possible. In moments of joy and struggle, prayer serves as our unwavering anchor. It connects us, heals us, and reminds us of our sacred commitment and vows to one another.

Each day of this devotional is designed to guide you in prayer, reflection, and connection. The Scripture Focus will ground you in God's truth, while the reflection questions will inspire meaningful conversations that foster intimacy and understanding. The guided prayers serve as a starting point, encouraging you to express your heart to God and to each other. Through the *"Our Story"* journaling section, you'll have the opportunity to document your journey, witnessing the ways God is working in your marriage.

I encourage the readers to approach this devotional with an open heart and a willingness to be vulnerable. Embrace the moments of joy, and allow God to speak to you in the moments of challenge. Remember that no marriage is perfect; it is the grace we extend to one another that leads to growth and deeper connection.

As you pray for one another, you are not only inviting God into your relationship but also nurturing a love that mirrors His. May this journey strengthen your bond and deepen your spiritual connection, allowing your marriage to flourish in His love.

I am incredibly proud of my dear brother and sister, Eric and Sherill, for staying the course to produce this remarkable body of work that will strengthen marriages, intertwine bonds, and mend hearts, all knitted together in love by the grace of Abba. You did it!!!

With Love and Prayers for Your Journey,

Pastor Allison Mahon

Introduction

Welcome to Praying for Our Spouses

Marriage is a beautiful, sacred gift from God—one that requires love, intentionality, and a foundation rooted in Him. As couples, we are called to reflect God's love, grace, and faithfulness in the way we love and serve one another. Yet, life can bring seasons of joy, trials, growth, and change that test the very bond we hold dear. Through it all, prayer becomes the anchor that keeps us grounded, connected, and filled with hope.

This devotional was written to help couples cultivate a habit of praying for one another daily. Whether you're newly married, have been together for decades, or are navigating a challenging season, this 31-day journey is designed to strengthen your spiritual bond as a couple and deepen your relationship with God. Each day includes:

- **A Scripture Focus:** A verse to meditate on and guide your thoughts for the day.
- **Reflection Questions:** Thoughtful prompts to encourage open communication and personal reflection.
- **A Guided Prayer:** A heartfelt prayer you can say together or individually.
- **Our Story:** A journaling section for you to record personal reflections, answered prayers, or milestones along your journey.

How to Use This Devotional

1. **Commit to Consistency:** Set aside time each day to pray and read together, whether in the morning, before bed, or during a quiet moment.
2. **Pray Together and Individually:** Use the guided prayer as a starting point but also speak from your heart. There's power in hearing each other's prayers and lifting up your spouse before God.
3. **Be Honest and Open:** Let the reflection questions spark deeper conversations. Vulnerability fosters connection.
4. **Journal Your Journey:** Take time to write in the "Our Story" section. This will become a beautiful testimony of God's work in your marriage.
5. **Extend Grace:** Remember that no marriage is perfect. Allow God to use this time to grow you closer, even when it feels challenging.

A Word of Encouragement

As you embark on this 31-day journey, know that God is for your marriage. He sees your joys, hears your prayers, and understands your struggles. You are not alone. Through prayer and His Word, God will strengthen your love, restore broken places, and guide you toward His perfect plan for your relationship.

Let this devotional be a sacred space where you and your spouse come together to invite God into your marriage—day by day, step by step, prayer by prayer.

May your hearts grow closer to each other and to the One who designed marriage for His glory.

With love and prayers,

Our Couples Pledge

Built on Faith. Bound by Love.
As husband and wife,
We pledge to keep Christ at the center of our marriage.
We will pray together, grow together, and face life hand in hand.
We will speak life, give grace, and extend forgiveness freely.
We will honor and cherish one another not just in the easy moments, but in the challenging ones too.
We commit to loving intentionally, dating consistently, and never giving up on the promise we made.
We will protect our union, cover each other in prayer, and build a home where God's love dwells richly.
We declare that marriage still works,
When it is rooted in faith,
sustained by love,
and covered by God's grace.
Together, we rise. Together, we thrive.
Forever linked by covenant, by purpose, and by God.
On _____, together, we make this pledge.

_____
Husband

_____
Wife

Day 1
A Foundation of Love

"And now these three remain: faith, hope, and love. But the greatest of these is love." **(1 Corinthians 13:13)**

Love is the foundation of every strong and enduring relationship. While faith anchors us in God's promises and hope gives us the strength to press forward, love is what binds it all together, reflecting God's perfect nature. In marriage, love is not merely an emotion but a daily choice to be patient, kind, and selfless, just as Christ loves us. As a couple, embracing this divine love allows you to weather challenges with grace and celebrate joys with gratitude. Remember that the greatest gift you can offer each other is a love that mirrors the unwavering, sacrificial love God has for us. Let this be the cornerstone of your union, as love truly is the greatest of all.

Reflection Questions
1. What does love look like in your marriage today?
2. How can you actively demonstrate love to your spouse this week?
3. In what ways can God's love transform areas of challenge in your relationship?

Prayer
Lord, thank You for the love You have shown us. Teach us to love as You love—patiently, selflessly, and unconditionally. Help us to see our spouses through Your eyes and strengthen the foundation of our marriage in Your perfect love. Amen.

Our Story
1. Reflect on a time when love carried your relationship through a challenge.
2. Write about ways you feel God's love is present in your marriage.
3. Include a prayer of gratitude for your spouse's love.

He Said...

She Said...

Day 2
Communication In Unity

"Let no corrupting talk come out of your mouths, but only such as is good for building up, as fits the occasion, that it may give grace to those who hear." (**Ephesians 4:29**)

Words are powerful—they have the ability to heal or harm, to build up or tear down. In marriage, the way we communicate can deeply affect the bond we share with our spouse. **Ephesians 4:29** reminds us to use our words thoughtfully, ensuring they are filled with grace and love, aimed at strengthening one another. When disagreements arise, choose words that promote understanding rather than division. Speak with kindness, even when addressing challenges, and encourage one another in your shared journey of faith. Let your conversations reflect God's love, creating an atmosphere where grace abounds and your hearts are drawn closer together.

Reflection Questions
1. How do your words build up or tear down your spouse?
2. What steps can you take to improve communication in your marriage?
3. How can prayer help you speak with grace and understanding?

Prayer
Lord, guide our words so they may bring unity and encouragement to our marriage. Help us listen with open hearts and respond with patience and kindness. May our communication reflect Your love. Amen.

Our Story
- Write about a meaningful conversation you've had with your spouse recently.
- Reflect on how improving communication has strengthened your relationship.

He Said...

She Said...

Day 3
Strengthening Trust

"Trust in the Lord with all your heart, and do not lean on your own understanding." (**Proverbs 3:5**)

Trust is essential in marriage, not only between spouses but also in your shared walk with God. **Proverbs 3:5** reminds us to place our full trust in the Lord, especially when facing uncertainty or challenges. As a couple, it can be tempting to rely on your own understanding or solutions, but true strength comes from surrendering to God's wisdom. Together, commit to seeking His guidance in prayer and allowing His plans to shape your journey. When you trust in Him with all your hearts, He will direct your steps and deepen your bond, filling your relationship with His peace and purpose.

Reflection Questions
1. What role does trust play in your marriage?
2. Are there areas where trust needs rebuilding or strengthening?
3. How can trusting God help you trust your spouse more deeply?

Prayer
Lord, thank You for being trustworthy in all things. Help us to grow in trust within our marriage. Give us the courage to be vulnerable and faithful to one another as we trust in You. Amen.

Our Story
- Reflect on a time when trust was tested in your marriage.
- Write about steps you and your spouse have taken to build or rebuild trust.

He Said...

She Said...

Day 4
Serving One Another

"For even the Son of Man came not to be served but to serve, and to give his life as a ransom for many." (**Mark 10:45**)

In marriage, Christ's example of selfless service becomes a powerful model for how we are called to love one another. **Mark 10:45** reminds us that Jesus came not to be served, but to serve and give His life for others. This same spirit of humility and sacrifice should define our relationships. True love is expressed through acts of service—putting your spouse's needs above your own, offering support, and nurturing one another in daily life. When both partners adopt this Christ-like mindset, it fosters a deeper connection rooted in mutual respect and love. Let your marriage reflect Jesus' heart, serving one another joyfully and selflessly as He serves us.

Reflection Questions
1. In what ways do you currently serve your spouse?
2. Are there areas where you can better serve their needs?
3. How does serving your spouse reflect God's love?

Prayer
Lord, thank You for Your example of sacrificial love. Teach us to serve one another with humility and joy. Help us to meet each other's needs and grow in love through service. Amen.

Our Story
- Write about a time when serving your spouse brought joy or healing.
- Reflect on how serving one another has deepened your bond.

He Said...

She Said...

Day 5
Praying for Wisdom

"If any of you lacks wisdom, you should ask God, who gives generously to all without finding fault, and it will be given to you".
(James 1:5)

Marriage is filled with decisions, both big and small, that require wisdom and discernment. **James 1:5** reminds us of God's promise to generously give wisdom to those who ask for it. As a couple, lean on this truth and seek God's guidance together in prayer when faced with challenges or uncertainties. Trust that He will provide clarity and direction as you navigate life's journey hand in hand. By inviting God into your decision-making, you not only grow in wisdom but also strengthen your unity and dependence on Him. Remember, His wisdom is perfect and will always lead you toward His good and loving plans.

Reflection Questions
1. In what areas do you need wisdom in your marriage?
2. How can you seek God's guidance together?
3. How does wisdom strengthen your relationship?

Prayer
Lord, grant us wisdom to navigate our marriage with grace. Help us to discern Your will and make choices that honor You and strengthen our union. Amen.

Our Story
- Reflect on a time when seeking wisdom together brought clarity or peace.

He Said...

She Said...

Day 6
Building Patience

"But the fruit of the Spirit is love, joy, peace, patience, kindness, goodness, faithfulness, gentleness, self-control; against such things there is no law". **(Galatians 5:22-23)**

The Fruit of the Spirit is a beautiful reflection of God's character, and it provides the foundation for a thriving marriage. These virtues are essential for building a strong and Christ-centered relationship. As a couple, invite the Holy Spirit to work within you, shaping your hearts and attitudes. When love overflows, joy abounds, and peace reigns, your marriage becomes a testimony of God's grace. Strive daily to nurture these fruits in your relationship. Let them guide your words, actions, and choices glorifying God in your union.

Reflection Questions
1. How can you show more patience in your marriage?
2. What challenges your patience, and how can you surrender it to God?
3. How does patience reflect Christ's love?

Prayer
Lord, grow patience within us so we can respond to one another with understanding and love. Teach us to wait on Your timing. Amen.

Our Story
- Reflect on a time when patience led to growth or reconciliation in your marriage.

He Said...

She Said...

Day 7
Embracing Forgiveness

"Bear with one another and forgive one another if anyone has a complaint against another; just as the Lord has forgiven you, so you also must forgive". (**Colossians 3:13**)

Forgiveness is a cornerstone of a healthy and lasting marriage. In marriage, there will be times of misunderstandings or hurt, but holding onto resentment only creates division. Instead, choose to extend grace and forgiveness, just as Christ has done for you. This act of love not only restores harmony but also deepens your connection with your spouse. Remember, forgiveness is not about forgetting but about choosing to move forward in love and unity. Let God's forgiveness inspire you to be patient and compassionate with each other, building a relationship that reflects His mercy and grace.

Reflection Questions
1. How can forgiveness bring healing to your relationship?
2. Are there areas where you need to forgive or seek forgiveness?
3. How does God's forgiveness inspire you to forgive?

Prayer
Lord, thank You for forgiving us. Teach us to forgive one another freely, as You have forgiven us. Heal any wounds in our marriage through grace. Amen.

Our Story
- Reflect on how forgiveness has played a role in your marriage.

He Said...

She Said...

WEEK 1
BUILDING A FOUNDATION OF LOVE

AFFIRMATION DAY
Write and exchange a note of encouragement, listing three things you admire about each other.

PRAYER WALK
Take a walk together and pray out loud, thanking God for each other.

MEMORY LANE
Share a favorite memory from your relationship and reflect on how God has brought you closer since then.

SILENT LOVE
Spend 10 minutes holding hands in silence, praying individually for your marriage.

DATE NIGHT-IN
Cook a meal together, set the table nicely, and enjoy an intentional dinner conversation.

SCRIPTURE SHARING
Share a Bible verse that reminds you of your spouse and explain why.

GRATITUDE JAR
Start a jar where you both write one thing you're thankful for in each other daily.

Day 8
Spiritual Growth Together

"For where two or three are gathered in my name, there am I in the midst of them" (**Matthew 18:20**)

This verse reminds us of the powerful presence of God when we come together in unity and prayer as a couple. No matter where we are or what challenges we face, gathering in His name invites His presence into our relationship. When we pray together, share our hearts, and seek His guidance, we ask God to be a central part of our marriage. His presence brings peace, healing, and strength. It reminds us that we are never alone in our journey together. Let this verse encourage you to make space for prayer, and know that God is with you both, walking alongside you in every season of your marriage.

Reflection Questions
1. How often do you pray together as a couple?
2. How can you prioritize spiritual growth in your marriage?
3. What blessings come from seeking God together?

Prayer
Lord, draw us closer to You and to one another. Help us grow spiritually and prioritize our relationship with You in our marriage. Amen.

Our Story
- Reflect on a moment of spiritual unity or growth in your marriage.

He Said...

She Said...

Day 9
Strength In Challenges

"I can do all things through Christ who strengthens me".
(Philippians 4:13)

As a couple, this powerful promise reminds us that we are never limited by our own strength. In moments of challenge, uncertainty, or even joy, we can rely on Christ to equip and empower us to face anything together. Whether it's managing the pressures of daily life, supporting each other through hardships, or celebrating victories, we don't have to do it on our own. Christ's strength is abundant, and His power makes all things possible. As you grow together, remember to lean on His limitless strength and trust that no matter what life brings, you can overcome with Him at your side.

Reflection Questions
1. What challenges are you facing in your marriage?
2. How can you rely on God's strength instead of your own?
3. How has God helped you overcome difficulties in the past?

Prayer
Lord, thank You for Your strength that sustains us. Help us face every challenge together with faith and courage. Amen.

Our Story
- Write about a challenge you've overcome together with God's help.

He Said...

She Said...

Day 10
Celebrating Differences

"For just as each of us has one body with many members, and these members do not all have the same function, so in Christ we, though many, form one body." **(Romans 12:4-5)**

In marriage, we are reminded that each of us brings unique gifts, strengths, and qualities to the relationship. Just as the body is made up of different parts that work together for a common purpose, so too is your marriage. You and your spouse are distinct individuals, yet you are united in Christ, called to work together as one. This verse encourages you to embrace each other's differences and strengths, knowing that you complement one another. Through teamwork, mutual respect, and love, you form a strong, unified bond. This reflects the unity that Christ desires for all His people.

Reflection Questions
1. How do your differences complement each other in marriage?
2. What are some ways you can appreciate your spouse's unique qualities?
3. How can you embrace differences instead of letting them divide you?

Prayer
Lord, thank You for creating us uniquely and for bringing us together as one. Teach us to celebrate our differences and see them as strengths in our marriage. Amen.

Our Story
- Reflect on a time when your differences worked together for good in your relationship.

He Said...

She Said...

Day 11
Growing In Gratitude

"Give thanks in all circumstances; for this is God's will for you in Christ Jesus." **(1 Thessalonians 5:18)**

This verse is a powerful reminder that gratitude is not just for the good times, but also for the challenges we face. In marriage, there will be moments of joy and moments of hardship. However, God calls us to cultivate an attitude of thanksgiving in every season. When you choose to thank God, even in difficult moments, you invite peace into your relationship. Gratitude helps you focus on God's faithfulness and provision, instead of dwelling on struggles. In marriage, express thankfulness not only for the easy moments but for the lessons and growth that come through the tough times. Trust that God's will for you and your spouse is to find joy in His presence, knowing that He works all things together for your good.

Reflection Questions
1. What are you most grateful for about your spouse?
2. How can showing gratitude strengthen your marriage?
3. In what ways can you express your gratitude daily?

Prayer
Lord, thank You for the gift of my spouse. Help me to see them through eyes of gratitude and express my appreciation often. Amen.

Our Story
- Write a note of gratitude for your spouse and reflect on their positive impact in your life.

He Said...

She Said...

Day 12
Facing Fears Together

"For God gave us a spirit not of fear but of power and love and self-control." **(2 Timothy 1:7)**

In marriage, it's easy to feel uncertain or fearful, especially when facing challenges or unfamiliar situations. However, this verse reminds us that God has not given us a spirit of fear, but one of power, love, and self-discipline. As a couple, you can face any circumstance with confidence, knowing that God's Spirit equips you both with strength and courage. His love empowers you to support each other and stay united through every trial, and His self-discipline helps you make wise choices that honor Him and each other. Let this verse be a reminder that you don't need to walk in fear or insecurity. Instead, lean on God's power and love to strengthen your relationship and face life's challenges together with boldness and grace.

Reflection Questions
1. What fears do you or your spouse face in your marriage?
2. How can you support each other in overcoming these fears?
3. How does God's presence give you courage?

Prayer
Lord, replace our fears with faith. Help us to face challenges boldly, knowing that You are with us and our marriage is in Your hands. Amen.

Our Story
- Reflect on a time when you and your spouse overcame a fear together.

He Said...

She Said...

Day 13
Financial Stewardship

"Honor the Lord with your wealth and with the first fruits of all your produce." **(Proverbs 3:9)**

This verse invites us to honor God with our resources, and as a couple, it can be a powerful reminder to put God first in every area of your life, including your finances. When you honor Him with your wealth, you acknowledge His provision and trust that He is the ultimate source of all that you have. This act of faith reflects your gratitude and commitment to His will, knowing that He is faithful to provide for all your needs. As you manage your finances together, remember to honor God with the first portion of what He blesses you with, whether it's through tithing, giving, or making wise financial decisions. By doing so, you invite God's blessings into your marriage and align your financial goals with His purposes, building a foundation of trust, unity, and generosity.

Reflection Questions
1. How do you approach finances as a couple?
2. What role does trust play in financial decisions?
3. How can you honor God through stewardship in your marriage?

Prayer
Lord, teach us to be wise and faithful stewards of the resources You've given us. Help us use our finances in ways that glorify You and bless our family. Amen.

Our Story
- Write about a financial decision you've made together and how it shaped your relationship.

He Said...

She Said...

Day 14
Protecting the Covenant

"Therefore what God has joined together, let no one separate."
(Mark 10:9)

This verse speaks to the sacredness and strength of the marriage covenant. In a world where relationships can often be tested by trials, distractions, and misunderstandings, it's important to remember that marriage is a bond established by God. He has brought you and your spouse together with a purpose, and that bond is meant to be unbreakable. When challenges arise, this verse encourages you to hold fast to each other and to God, trusting that He is the one who strengthens and sustains your union. Let this verse serve as a reminder that your marriage is not just a human contract but a divine commitment. Honor it by working through difficulties together, protecting the unity that God has ordained, and building a relationship that reflects His love and faithfulness.

Reflection Questions
1. How do you guard your marriage against external challenges?
2. What steps can you take to protect the sacredness of your covenant?
3. How can prayer serve as a safeguard for your relationship?

Prayer
Lord, thank You for joining us together as one. Help us to honor and protect the covenant of our marriage, keeping You at the center always. Amen.

Our Story
- Reflect on a time when you intentionally protected your marriage from outside influences.

He Said...

She Said...

WEEK 11
STRENGTHENING COMMUNICATION

LISTENING EXERCISE
Take turns sharing how you're feeling about life right now. No interruptions—just listen.

LOVE LANGUAGES CHECK-IN
Discuss your love languages and brainstorm ways to meet each other's needs.

PRAYER SWAP
Write a short prayer for each other and swap them to read privately.

NO PHONES NIGHT
Dedicate an evening to being fully present with no screens or interruptions.

QUESTION JAR
Write 5 open-ended questions each, put them in a jar, and take turns drawing and answering them.

STORY SWAP
Share something about your childhood that your spouse might not know.

ENCOURAGEMENT BOARD
Create a list of affirmations, dreams, and prayers you have for your marriage.

Week III
Renewing Togetherness

Day 15
Renewing Commitment

"Commit to the Lord whatever you do, and He will establish your plans." **(Proverbs 16:3)**

This verse encourages us to bring everything—our dreams, our goals, our marriage—before God. When you and your spouse commit your plans to the Lord, you invite His guidance, wisdom, and blessing into your lives. No matter what you face, when you put God at the center of your efforts, He directs your steps and helps you navigate both the easy and challenging seasons. In marriage, this means seeking God's will in all decisions, big or small, trusting that He will provide the strength and clarity needed. By dedicating your plans to Him, you demonstrate faith that He will establish your relationship, guide your future, and empower you both to fulfill the purpose He has for your marriage. Let your commitment to God strengthen the foundation of your life together, knowing that He will faithfully lead you.

Reflection Questions
1. What does commitment mean to you in your marriage?
2. How can you renew your vows to each other daily?
3. In what ways can you commit your marriage to God?

Prayer
Lord, help us to renew our commitment to You and to each other daily. May our words, actions, and love reflect the vows we made before You. Amen.

Our Story
- Write about why you committed to your spouse and how you continue to uphold that commitment.

He Said...

She Said...

Day 16
Walking In Faith Together

"For we walk by faith, not by sight." **(2 Corinthians 5:7)**

Let this verse encourage you to walk by faith. Know that God is with you every step of the way, even when the road seems unclear. But this verse reminds us that our journey is guided by faith, not by our circumstances. As a couple, it's important to trust God even when the path ahead seems uncertain. Living by faith means relying on His promises, His timing, and His plans, rather than trying to control every detail. Trusting God's direction for your marriage, even when you can't see the full picture, deepens your bond and strengthens your trust in Him. Let this verse encourage you to walk by faith, knowing that God is with you every step of the way, even when the road seems unclear. Your trust in Him will lead to growth, peace, and a deeper connection in your relationship.

Reflection Questions
1. How can you encourage each other to live by faith?
2. What steps of faith can you take as a couple?
3. How does trusting God bring peace to your marriage?

Prayer
Lord, help us walk by faith and trust in Your promises. May our faith in You strengthen our bond and guide our marriage. Amen.

Our Story
- Reflect on a time when you trusted God together and saw Him work in your lives.

He Said...

She Said...

Day 17
Encouraging One Another

"Therefore encourage one another and build one another up, just as you are doing." **(1 Thessalonians 5:11)**

In marriage, encouragement is a powerful tool that strengthens and sustains your relationship. This verse reminds us that we are called to lift each other up, especially during challenging times. When you encourage your spouse, you are building them up, affirming their worth, and supporting their growth. Whether it's through kind words, acts of service, or simply being present, your encouragement can be a constant source of strength and hope. Let this verse challenge you to be intentional in your words and actions, offering love and affirmation to each other daily. As you do, you will create an environment of trust, respect, and mutual support, where both of you can thrive in your marriage.

Reflection Questions
1. How can you encourage your spouse in their daily life?
2. What words or actions have encouraged you recently?
3. How does encouragement build trust and intimacy?

Prayer
Lord, let us be each other's greatest encouragers. Teach us to speak life, build confidence, and lift each other up in all circumstances. Amen.

Our Story
- Write about a moment when encouragement made a difference in your marriage.

He Said...

She Said...

Day 18
Protecting Your Hearts

"Above all else, guard your heart, for everything you do flows from it." **(Proverbs 4:23)**

This verse highlights the importance of protecting your heart, as it is the wellspring of your actions, thoughts, and decisions. In marriage, the health of your heart directly impacts the health of your relationship. Guarding your heart means being mindful of what you allow to influence your emotions, thoughts, and attitudes. It also means nurturing love, patience, and forgiveness within your heart so that your words and actions reflect God's love for your spouse. When you protect your heart from negativity, bitterness, and unforgiveness, you allow the Holy Spirit to work in you, strengthening your marriage and fostering deeper intimacy. Take time to reflect on what you're allowing into your heart and intentionally choose to fill it with love, grace, and God's truth, so that your relationship can flourish.

Reflection Questions
1. How can you guard your spouse's heart in daily interactions?
2. Are there areas where you need to protect your own heart from hurt or negativity?
3. How does inviting God into your heart bring peace to your marriage?

Prayer
Lord, help us protect each other's hearts with love and understanding. Guard our hearts and minds so that everything we do reflects Your goodness. Amen.

Our Story
- Reflect on how you've nurtured emotional safety in your marriage.

He Said...

She Said...

Day 19
Honoring Each Other

"Be devoted to one another in love. Honor one another above yourselves." **(Romans 12:10)**

In marriage, this verse calls us to practice sacrificial love and mutual respect. Being devoted to one another means putting your spouse's needs and well-being above your own, consistently choosing to love and serve them. Honor, in this context, is about valuing your spouse, recognizing their worth, and treating them with dignity and care. It's easy to take each other for granted, but this verse reminds us that honoring your spouse is a continual choice that strengthens the bond between you. By serving each other with a selfless heart, you create an environment where love flourishes, and the relationship grows deeper. Let this verse inspire you to daily express your devotion and honor to your spouse, building a marriage that reflects Christ's love and commitment to us.

Reflection Questions
1. How do you honor your spouse in your words and actions?
2. What are practical ways you can prioritize and respect each other?
3. How does honoring one another reflect God's love?

Prayer
Lord, teach us to honor one another in love. Help us to put each other first and treat our marriage with reverence and care. Amen.

Our Story
- Reflect on a time when you or your spouse felt truly honored.

He Said...

She Said...

Day 20
Loving Through Challenges

"Be completely humble and gentle; be patient, bearing with one another in love." **(Ephesians 4:2)**

In marriage, humility, gentleness, and patience are key to fostering a healthy, loving relationship. This verse reminds us that being humble means putting aside pride and ego. We can serve and support our spouse with a heart of compassion. Gentleness means responding with kindness and understanding, even when emotions are high or disagreements arise. Patience allows us to endure the imperfections and mistakes of our spouse, recognize that as a couple we are on a journey of growth. Bearing with one another in love means showing grace when challenges arise and choosing to love unconditionally. In your marriage, let these qualities guide your interactions, helping you build a foundation of respect, trust, and unconditional love that reflects Christ's character.

Reflection Questions
1. What challenges are testing your marriage right now?
2. How can love and patience help you navigate these struggles?
3. How has God's love sustained you through difficulties?

Prayer
Lord, strengthen us to love each other through trials. Grant us humility, patience, and grace as we face challenges together. Amen.

Our Story
- Write about how your love has grown through seasons of hardship.

He Said...

She Said...

Day 21
Restoring Joy

"The joy of the Lord is your strength." **(Nehemiah 8:10)**

In marriage, there will inevitably be moments of difficulty, disappointment, or even sorrow. However, this verse reminds us that God's joy can be a powerful source of strength in those times. Even when things seem tough, His joy is not dependent on our circumstances but on His faithfulness and presence in our lives. As a couple, when you lean on God's joy, it strengthens you both, providing peace and resilience to face challenges together. Let the joy of the Lord be a foundation in your marriage, especially when life feels heavy. By focusing on His goodness and trusting in His strength, you will find the courage to press forward and experience renewed hope and unity, knowing that God is with you, sustaining your relationship through every season.

Reflection Questions
1. What brings joy to your marriage?
2. How can you bring laughter and happiness into daily life?
3. How does God's joy sustain you during tough times?

Prayer
Lord, restore and renew joy in our marriage. Let laughter and peace fill our home as we delight in You and each other. Amen.

Our Story
- Reflect on moments of joy and fun in your relationship and how they've drawn you closer.

He Said...

She Said...

WEEK III
RENEWING TOGETHERNESS BUILDING TRUST AND INTIMACY

HEART CHECK-IN
Ask, "What's one thing I can do this week to make you feel more loved?"

COUPLE'S DEVOTIONAL NIGHT
Read a passage from the devotional and journal together about its impact.

30-SECOND HUG
Commit to hugging each other for 30 seconds daily, even if life feels hectic.

SURPRISE GESTURE
Do something small but meaningful for your spouse (e.g., make their favorite snack, leave a note in their car).

DREAM TOGETHER
Spend time sharing your goals and dreams for the next year or beyond.

COUPLE'S PLAYLIST
Create a playlist of songs that remind you of each other or your journey together.

CANDLELIGHT CONVERSATION
Light candles and talk about your favorite moments in your relationship so far.

Day 22
Cultivating Peace

"Blessed are the peacemakers, for they will be called children of God."
(Matthew 5:9)

In marriage, being a peacemaker means actively pursuing reconciliation, understanding, and harmony, especially during times of conflict. This verse challenges us to reflect God's heart by striving for peace, not only by avoiding arguments but by working to restore peace when it is disrupted. A peacemaker listens with empathy, seeks common ground, and chooses forgiveness over holding onto grudges. When both partners embrace this role, your marriage becomes a witness of God's love and grace. Remember, peace is not the absence of conflict, but the presence of love, patience, and humility in the midst of it. Let this verse inspire you to be intentional about creating peace in your home, allowing God to work through your efforts to build a relationship that reflects His heart.

Reflection Questions
1. What disrupts peace in your relationship?
2. How can you actively work toward resolving conflicts?
3. How does inviting God's peace change your marriage?

Prayer
Lord, make us peacemakers in our home. Help us to approach disagreements with patience and a heart for reconciliation. Amen.

Our Story
- Write about a time when peace prevailed in a challenging situation.

He Said...

She Said...

Day 23
Nurturing Intimacy

"Let him kiss me with the kisses of his mouth—for your love is more delightful than wine." **(Song of Solomon 1:2)**

This verse expresses a deep longing for intimate connection and love, celebrating the passionate and affectionate nature of a relationship. In marriage, this verse can remind us of the beauty of keeping romance and affection alive. Just as wine brings delight, the love shared between a husband and wife should be cherished and cultivated, creating moments of closeness and joy. The intimate connection that is described here goes beyond physical attraction; it speaks to the depth of emotional and spiritual intimacy that strengthens the bond between you and your spouse. Let this verse inspire you to continually nurture the love in your marriage, to enjoy each other's presence, and to remind one another of the beauty of the relationship you share.

Reflection Questions
1. How do you nurture emotional and physical intimacy in your marriage?
2. What role does vulnerability play in deepening your bond?
3. How can prayer invite God into the intimate areas of your relationship?

Prayer
Lord, draw us closer together in love and intimacy. Help us to connect deeply in ways that reflect Your design for marriage. Amen.

Our Story
- Reflect on moments of intimacy that have strengthened your connection.

He Said...

She Said...

Day 24
Trusting God's Timing

"There is a time for everything, and a season for every activity under the heavens." **(Ecclesiastes 3:1)**

This verse reminds us that life, including our marriage, is filled with different seasons—each with its own purpose and timing. There will be times of joy, growth, and excitement, as well as seasons of difficulty, challenge, and change. As a couple, embracing the truth that every season has a purpose helps you navigate life's ups and downs with grace and trust in God's perfect timing. Whether you are in a season of rest, hard work, raising children, or rebuilding, know that God is present in each moment, guiding you both through it. Trust that each season will shape and strengthen your marriage, making it more resilient and deeply rooted in love. Embrace the season you are in, knowing that God is at work, and He will lead you through each phase of your life together.

Reflection Questions

1. Are there areas in your marriage where you need to trust God's timing?
2. How can you remain patient and faithful while waiting on His plan?
3. What past moments remind you of God's perfect timing?

Prayer

Lord, help us trust in Your perfect timing for every season of our marriage. Teach us patience and remind us that Your plans are always good. Amen.

Our Story

- Write about a time when God's timing brought blessings to your marriage.

He Said...

She Said...

Day 25
Faithfulness In All Things

"Let love and faithfulness never leave you; bind them around your neck, write them on the tablet of your heart." **(Proverbs 3:3)**

In marriage, love and faithfulness are the foundation that strengthens the relationship. This verse calls us to hold these virtues close, keeping them at the center of our actions, thoughts, and attitudes. Love is what drives us to care for and cherish our spouse, while faithfulness is the commitment to stand by them, through all circumstances. By *"binding them around your neck"* and *"writing them on your heart,"* you're committing to making love and faithfulness central to your marriage. It means choosing to love unconditionally and remain loyal, even when challenges arise. Let this verse be a reminder to guard and nurture these qualities, creating a bond that is unbreakable, rooted in God's love and faithfulness toward you both.

Reflection Questions
1. How do you show faithfulness to your spouse in daily life?
2. Are there areas where you can grow in faithfulness?
3. How does faithfulness reflect God's covenant love?

Prayer
Lord, thank You for Your unwavering faithfulness. Teach us to be faithful to each other in thought, word, and action. May our commitment mirror Your steadfast love. Amen.

Our Story
- Reflect on a moment where faithfulness strengthened your relationship.

He Said...

She Said...

Day 26
Healing Through Prayer

"Therefore confess your sins to each other and pray for each other so that you may be healed. The prayer of a righteous person is powerful and effective." **(James 5:16)**

This verse highlights the importance of vulnerability, trust, and prayer in strengthening a marriage. Confessing your faults and weaknesses to one another builds a foundation of honesty and transparency, allowing you to grow closer as you support each other in love. Prayer becomes a powerful tool for healing, bringing both comfort and strength, as you turn to God together, lifting up your concerns, needs, and praises. The "prayer of a righteous person" described here is one filled with faith, hope, and love, and when offered, it has the ability to bring profound change and renewal. Let this verse encourage you to create a space of trust in your marriage where you can openly share, pray, and rely on God's power to bring healing and wholeness.

Reflection Questions
1. What areas of your marriage need healing?
2. How can prayer bring emotional, spiritual, or physical restoration?
3. How does praying for each other deepen your connection?

Prayer
Lord, we ask for Your healing touch in every area of our marriage. Strengthen us through prayer, and help us extend grace and compassion to one another. Amen.

Our Story
- Write about a time when prayer brought healing or comfort in your marriage.

He Said...

She Said...

Day 27
Strengthening Unity

"Make every effort to keep the unity of the Spirit through the bond of peace." **(Ephesians 4:3)**

In marriage, unity is essential for a strong and lasting relationship. This verse encourages us to actively work to preserve the harmony and oneness that God desires for us. It's not always easy to maintain peace, especially when disagreements arise, but this verse reminds us that keeping the unity of the Spirit is a priority. It requires humility, patience, and a willingness to put aside our desires for the good of the relationship. The bond of peace holds a marriage together, allowing love to flourish and strengthen your connection. Let this verse be a reminder to make every effort to be gentle, kind, and understanding with one another, seeking reconciliation and working to protect the peace and unity that God has entrusted to you both.

Reflection Questions
1. What does unity look like in your marriage?
2. Are there specific actions or attitudes that threaten your oneness?
3. How can you invite God to strengthen the bond of unity in your relationship?

Prayer
Lord, help us walk in unity as a couple. We must prioritize peace and harmony in our marriage and seek You in all we do. Amen.

Our Story
- Reflect on a moment when unity allowed you to overcome a challenge together.

He Said...

She Said...

Day 28
Overcoming Temptations

"No temptation has overtaken you except what is common to mankind. And God is faithful; He will not let you be tempted beyond what you can bear. But when you are tempted, He will also provide a way out so that you can endure it." **(1 Corinthians 10:13)**

In marriage, there will be moments of temptation—whether it's through personal struggles, external pressures, or challenges within the relationship. This verse is a reminder that in every situation, God is faithful and will never allow you to face more than you can handle. He will always provide a way out, offering strength, wisdom, and peace when you need it most. As a couple, this verse encourages you to support one another through tough times, reminding each other of God's faithfulness. Trust that no temptation or challenge is too great, and together, with God's help, you can navigate any difficulty, emerging stronger in your faith and in your marriage.

Reflection Questions
1. What temptations do you face that could impact your marriage?
2. How can you work together to guard against these challenges?
3. How can God's faithfulness help you overcome temptation?

Prayer
Lord, protect our marriage from temptations that threaten to divide us. Give us the strength to resist and the wisdom to seek Your way out. Amen.

Our Story
- Write about how you and your spouse have supported each other in overcoming challenges or temptations.

He Said...

She Said...

WEEK IV

JESUS THE THIRD CORD
WALKING IN FAITH TOGETHER

SERVE TOGETHER
Find a small way to serve others as a team (e.g., donate to a food pantry, deliver a meal).

PRAYER PARTNERS
Take turns praying for each other's specific needs before bed.

WORSHIP NIGHT
Sing or listen to worship songs together and discuss which lyrics stand out to you.

BIBLE VERSE ART
Write or design your favorite scripture on a card or canvas to display in your home.

GRATITUDE PRAYER
Thank God together for 10 specific blessings in your marriage.

CHURCH INVOLVEMENT
Volunteer to serve in a ministry or attend a church event as a couple.

BLESS A FRIEND
Pray for another couple and think of a way to encourage them.

Day 29
Leaving A Legacy of Love

"These commandments that I give you today are to be on your hearts. Impress them on your children. Talk about them when you sit at home and when you walk along the road, when you lie down and when you get up." **(Deuteronomy 6:6-7)**

This passage highlights the importance of making God's Word central to your daily life and relationship. It's not just about reading scripture or having a moment of devotion—it's about letting His commandments shape everything you do. As a couple, you are called to embody and share these teachings, not just through words but through actions. Whether you're at home, on a walk, or at the beginning and end of each day, let God's truth guide your interactions, decisions, and conversations. This verse also encourages you to pass on these values to your children, teaching them by example the importance of living with God at the center. By continually seeking His guidance, you create a foundation of faith that strengthens your marriage and impacts future generations.

Reflection Questions
1. What kind of legacy do you want to leave as a couple?
2. How do your words and actions model love for future generations?
3. How can you honor God in the way you build your family and community?

Prayer
Lord, guide us as we leave a legacy of love and faith for those around us. May our marriage inspire others to see Your goodness. Amen.

Our Story
- Reflect on the ways your marriage impacts your children, family, or community.

He Said...

She Said...

Day 30
Renewing Hope

"For I know the plans I have for you," declares the Lord, "plans to prosper you and not to harm you, plans to give you hope and a future." **(Jeremiah 29:11)**

In marriage, this verse offers comfort and assurance that God has a purpose for your relationship. No matter what challenges or uncertainties you face, trust that God's plans for you and your spouse are filled with hope and goodness. His desire is to see your marriage flourish, to grow you both closer to Him and to each other. Even when life feels uncertain or difficult, this verse reminds you that God is in control and is working everything for your good. Let this truth encourage you to surrender your future to Him, knowing that He will guide you and provide all you need to build a strong, loving, and lasting marriage. Keep trusting His plan and remember that the hope He gives will sustain you through every season of life together.

Reflection Questions
1. How does hope shape the way you approach your marriage?
2. Are there areas where you need to renew hope in God's promises?
3. How can focusing on God's plans bring peace to your relationship?

Prayer
Lord, thank You for the hope You provide for our marriage. Renew our trust in Your plans and help us move forward with faith and joy. Amen.

Our Story
- Write about a time when hope in God's promises renewed your strength as a couple.

He Said...

She Said...

Day 31
A Prayer of Blessing

"The Lord bless you and keep you; the Lord make His face shine on you and be gracious to you; the Lord turn His face toward you and give you peace." **(Numbers 6:24-26)**

This powerful blessing speaks to the heart of God's love and care for His people, and it is especially meaningful in marriage. As a couple, you can claim these blessings over your relationship and trust that God will bless and protect you, and shine His favor upon you. The phrase *"The Lord make his face shine on you"* symbolizes God's approval, joy, and presence in your lives. His grace and peace are available to you, strengthening your bond and guiding you through both joyful and challenging times. This blessing is not just for moments of celebration, but also in times of struggle to remind you that God's love is constant and His presence is with you. As you seek God together, allow His blessing to fill your marriage with grace, joy, peace, and deep love.

Reflection Questions
1. How has God blessed your marriage so far?
2. In what ways can you be a blessing to your spouse?
3. How can you pray for God's continued blessing over your relationship?

Prayer
Lord, we thank You for Your blessings in our marriage. Shine Your face upon us, guide our steps, and fill our hearts with peace and love. May our union glorify You always. Amen.

Our Story
- Reflect on the greatest blessings you've experienced in your marriage and write a prayer of thanksgiving.

He Said...

She Said...

WEEK V

FORGIVENESS EXERCISE
Reflect on any unresolved hurt and ask for or extend forgiveness if needed.

MARRIAGE VISION BOARD
Create a visual board with pictures, words, and scriptures that represent your future goals.

COUPLE'S COMMITMENT LETTER
Write down a prayer or letter committing to continue growing in love, grace, and faith together.

Endorsements

"This devotional is a valuable resource for strengthening marriages, provided both partners commit to engaging with each lesson. The reflection questions encourage meaningful dialogue, fostering improved communication between spouses.

The lesson on serving one another particularly stands out, creating opportunities to deepen the marital bond through intentional acts of service. Additionally, the prayer time at the end of each devotion serves as a thoughtful and impactful way to close each session, further enhancing the couple's connection. Definitely a devotional that each couple should invest in."

Pastor Tim and Elder Nathalie Grant

"The Carpenters are considerate in their writing style. Their passion for God's people shows from their practical yet encouraging teachings that give opportunity for reflection and change that ignite closeness and the kind of vulnerability that makes marriages last."

Minister William and Elder Kishia Millhouse

You Must be Willing to Put in the WORK!

From game nights and time with our children to laughing and crying together, we have had a front row seat in the life of the Carpenter's for many years. However, it was through the couple's fellowships we hosted that we truly became knitted together. They would attend when things were great, and just as importantly, they would attend when things were not so great. They were willing to put in the work to make their marriage last. Willing to put in the work to be happy. Willing to put in the work for their children. Willing to put in the work for each other. Most importantly, they were willing to put in the work because the word of God commands us to.

This book reflects the work that the Carpenters have put into their marriage and there is no point in reading it unless you and your spouse are ready to do the same. To your benefit, it's designed for you to take your time, read, pray, and reflect on what you have read together. Pastor Andrea and I highly recommend that you take it one day and one page at a time; write and share your hearts with each other. You will be surprised at what's revealed through the words you take in and the work that you put in.

Rev's. Keith & Andrea Heyward

Senior Pastors, Dabar Christian Center, Chesapeake, VA
Marriage Counselors & Conference Facilitators

About the Authors

Eric Carpenter

is a family man. He is a loving, doting husband and father to four daughters, one son and a granddaughter. He also has many spiritual sons and daughters. Eric serves as Head Deacon and Armor bearer to his father in love Bishop Easton Grant at the New Life Open Bible Church in Springfield, VA,

Eric and his wife Sherill have counseled and supported many couples through their most difficult seasons. He co-authored this devotional with absolute joy to encourage godly marriages. Eric believes it is important for couples to spend time together in the Word of God and in prayer. It is out of this lived experience that he and his wife Sherill are founders of Forever Linked a couples ministry. -Built on Faith. Bound by Love.

About the Authors

Sherill Grant-Carpenter

is a woman after God's own heart, a passionate worshipper and servant, committed to advancing the Kingdom and fulfilling her divine assignment. Alongside her husband, Eric Carpenter, she co-founded Forever Linked, a couples ministry dedicated to counseling and supporting marriages through life's most challenging seasons. Together, they stand firm in the belief that marriage still works. Sherill boldly declares that her own marriage is Built on Faith. Bound by Love, and desires to see other couples thrive and endure.

Sherill is deeply devoted to all things "Family." She is a proud wife, a loving mother of three biological children and two bonus children, and a committed daughter who serves alongside her parents, Bishop Easton and the late Dr. Joy Grant, at New Life Open Bible Church in Springfield, VA.

In addition to her ministry work, Sherill is a licensed Mental Health Therapist and Social Worker, uniquely equipped to support individuals—especially youth—navigating emotional, psychological, and spiritual challenges. Her heart for community healing is evident in her nonprofit, Sherill Grant-Carpenter Ministries (SGCM), which empowers and uplifts women and girls through mental health education, job readiness training, conflict resolution classes, and self-worth workshops that combat suicide and hopelessness. SGCM currently supports local shelters and continues to expand its reach and impact.

Sherill's most recent divine assignment is Pray for Our Girls, a powerful call to action for mothers, godmothers, grandmothers, aunties, and women of all generations to gather in intercession for the next generation. She leads this prayer initiative live on Facebook every Tuesday at 7 PM, featuring guest intercessors who join the fight for wisdom, guidance, and spiritual clarity for our girls as they journey through life and toward eternity.

Wherever Sherill goes, she brings healing, hope, and the heart of a servant. And with so much more on the horizon, her story is still being written.

Stay tuned...

JOIN THE FOREVER LINKED ONLINE COMMUNITY!

WWW.SGCMINISTRIES.COM
@FOREVERLINKED

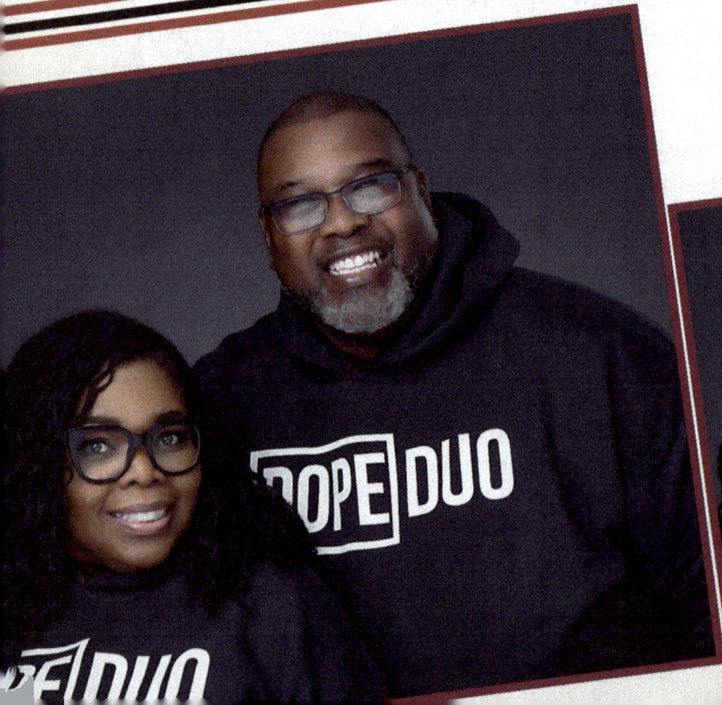

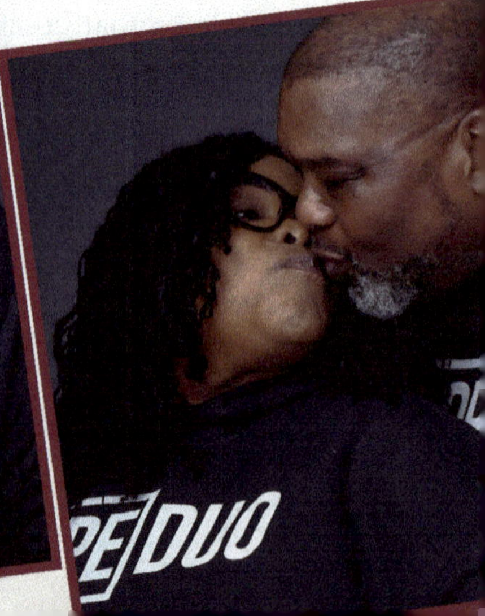

From the Publisher

GREAT BOOKS
ARE EVEN BETTER WHEN THEY'RE SHARED!

HELP OTHER READERS FIND THIS ONE:

- Post reviews at your favorite online booksellers

- Post a picture on your social media accounts and share why you enjoyed it

- Send a note to a friend or colleague who would also love it-or better yet, gift them a copy!

Thanks for reading!

www.ingramcontent.com/pod-product-compliance
Lightning Source LLC
Chambersburg PA
CBHW051946160426
43198CB00013B/2325